SUPER
TRUCKS

Author:

Ian Graham was born
in Belfast in 1953. He studied
applied physics at The City
University, London, and took
a postgraduate diploma in
journalism at the same
university, specialising in
science and technology
journalism. After four years
as an editor of consumer
electronics magazines, he
became a freelance author and
journalist. Since then, he has
written more than one hundred
children's non-fiction books and
numerous magazine articles.

Artist:

Nick Hewetson was
born in Surrey in 1958. He was
educated in Sussex at Brighton
Technical School and studied
illustration at Eastbourne
College of Art. He has since
illustrated a wide variety of
children's books.

Editor:

Jamie Pitman

Editorial Assistant:

Mark Williams

Published in Great Britain in MMIX by
Book House, an imprint of
The Salariya Book Company Ltd
25 Marlborough Place, Brighton, BNI IUB
www.salariya.com
www.book-house.co.uk

PB ISBN 978-1-906714-55-0

SALARIYA

A CIP Catalogue record for this book is available
from the British Library.

Printed and bound in China.
Printed on paper from sustainable sources.

**PAPER FROM
SUSTAINABLE
FORESTS**

Visit our website at www.book-house.co.uk
for **free** electronic versions of:
You Wouldn't Want to be an Egyptian Mummy!
You Wouldn't Want to be a Roman Gladiator!
Avoid Joining Shackleton's Polar Expedition!
Avoid Sailing on a 19th-Century Whaling Ship!

This book is adapted from *Super
Trucks* by Ian Graham, created,
designed and produced by The
Salariya Book Company and
published by Hodder Wayland in
MMI in the Fast Forward series.

SUPER TRUCKS

Written by
IAN GRAHAM

Illustrated by
NICK HEWETSON

Created and designed by
DAVID SALARIYA

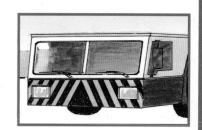

Contents

6

The First Trucks
From 'horseless carriages' to motor trucks.

8

Trucks for Tasks
A variety of trucks on the roads today and their uses.

10

Truck Racing
The fastest and most powerful trucks on the racetrack.

13

Construction Trucks
Trucks that shift concrete and other building materials.

14

Articulated Trucks
The biggest goods-carrying trucks in existence.

18

Tippers and Dumpers
From dump trucks and skip trucks to forklifts, wreckers and dustbin lorries.

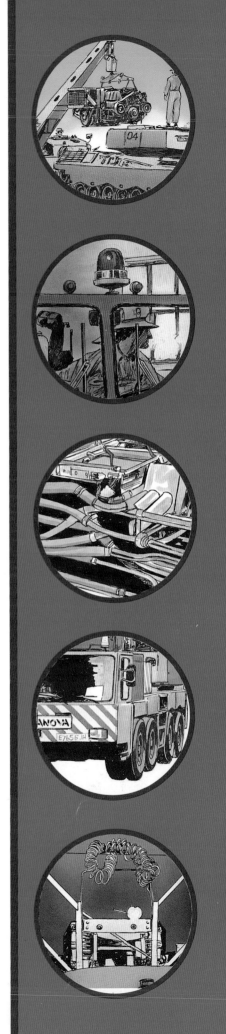

22

Military Trucks
Trucks that transport soldiers and weapons.

24

Fire Engines
From hand-operated water pumps on wheels
to the 'super' engines of today.

26

Road Trains
The longest trucks in the world.

28

Trucks to Come
Designs and technology for the
trucks of the future.

30

Useful Words

31

Milestones

32

Index

The First Trucks

1898 Daimler

The first trucks were steam-powered machines. They belched black smoke. By the 1890s, petrol-driven trucks were a great improvement. But they were not comfortable to drive. The **cab** gave little shelter and the solid rubber tyres gave quite a hard, bumpy ride.

▲ Early trucks were just a motorised platform with a seat. The first motor truck was built in 1896.

◄ The Autocar '2 Tons' could carry two tonnes in weight. Autocar is one of the oldest makes of trucks in America.

1926 Autocar 2 Tons

*1911
Lacre*

*1926
Chevrolet*

▲ By the 1920s, trucks looked less like carriages and more like today's motor trucks.

▲ The British Lacre had wooden wheels and rubber tyres like a horse-drawn carriage.

▶ This truck is fitted with metal wheels and **pneumatic** tyres.

1931 Chevrolet

At one time, all trucks had to be loaded and unloaded by hand. They spent less time on the roads.

Trucks for Tasks

Trucks are used to carry **freight** by road. They are built onto a steel frame called a **chassis**. Most trucks are powered by **diesel** engines. They are stronger and less expensive than petrol engines. Some trucks are equipped with machinery, such as a **winch**, to pull things on board.

Airport tug

▶ Some recovery trucks have a platform that tilts down to the ground. Cars can be winched up onto it.

▼ Trucks that tow trailers behind them can carry more. This is called a drawbar-trailer outfit.

Drawbar-trailer outfit

Heavy truck

Tanker

▲ Tankers transport liquids. They deliver petrol to fuel stations and liquid chemicals to manufacturers.

◀ Tow trucks pick up cars that have broken down or have been in accidents.

Winch

Tow truck

8

Airport tugs are vehicles used to move aircraft. Most of the vehicle is taken up by its powerful engine, with a small driver's cab at the front. It can fit underneath an airliner's nose and hook up to its nose wheel to tow it.

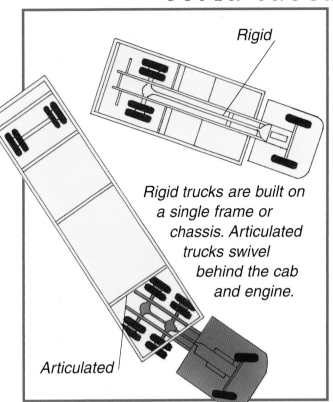

Rigid

Rigid trucks are built on a single frame or chassis. Articulated trucks swivel behind the cab and engine.

Articulated

Recovery truck

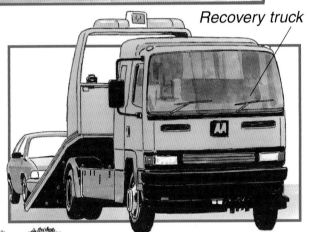

▼ Delivery trucks are smaller than heavy trucks. They carry smaller loads over shorter distances.

Delivery truck

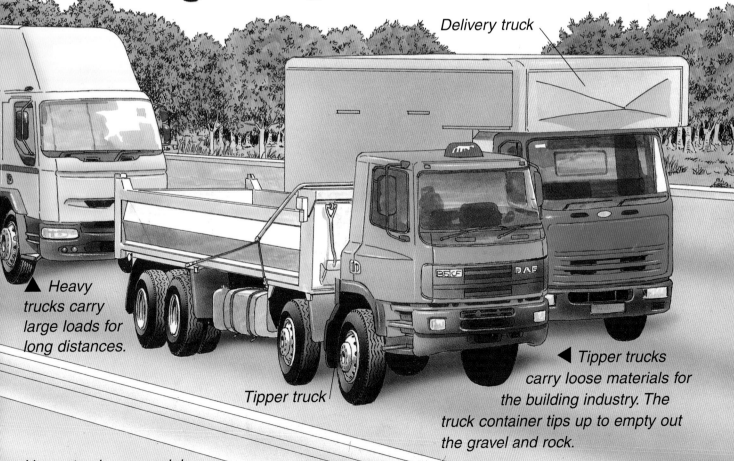

▲ Heavy trucks carry large loads for long distances.

Tipper truck

◄ Tipper trucks carry loose materials for the building industry. The truck container tips up to empty out the gravel and rock.

Heavy trucks can weigh over 40,000 kg.

Truck Racing

Trucks are unlikely racing vehicles, but many high-speed trucks are raced. Pick-up trucks and articulated **tractor** units are just as powerful as many racing cars.

▼ Racing cars and their teams travel to races in giant trailers. Inside is a car workshop and a kitchen, lounge and shower for the team.

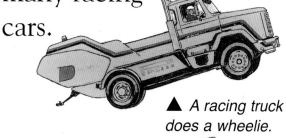

▲ *A racing truck does a wheelie.*

▶ *Monster trucks try to outdo each other climbing over obstacles and doing wheelies.*

▼ *Craftsman trucks draw large crowds at NASCAR races in the USA.*

▶ *Racing trucks race for the first corner. They are driven in the same way as racing cars.*

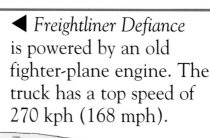

◀ *Freightliner Defiance* is powered by an old fighter-plane engine. The truck has a top speed of 270 kph (168 mph).

▲ *International Endeavor III* is a special truck designed to set speed records. Its engine is five times more powerful than a normal road truck.

▶ A concrete-mixer's drum has curved **vanes** inside it. When the drum turns, the vanes keep the concrete moving. This stops the concrete from setting.

Construction Trucks

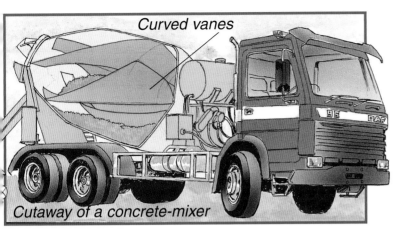

Curved vanes

Cutaway of a concrete-mixer

T he construction industry depends on heavy trucks to carry its building materials. Concrete-mixer trucks are always needed. Small trucks called dump trucks have a large bucket to carry materials around construction sites.

▼ At the building site, the drum turns the other way. This feeds the concrete down a chute.

Chute

Road crane truck

A truck can have all sorts of machinery added to it. This truck has a crane made of sections that slide inside each other. This makes it easy to transport.

Articulated Trucks

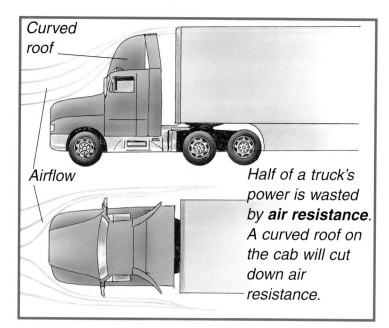

Curved roof

Airflow

Half of a truck's power is wasted by **air resistance**. A curved roof on the cab will cut down air resistance.

Articulated trucks have a swivel joint behind the driver's cab. This makes it easier for the truck to turn. The loaded part of the truck can be taken off. A new load can then be added.

Tractor unit

Semi-trailer

Air filter

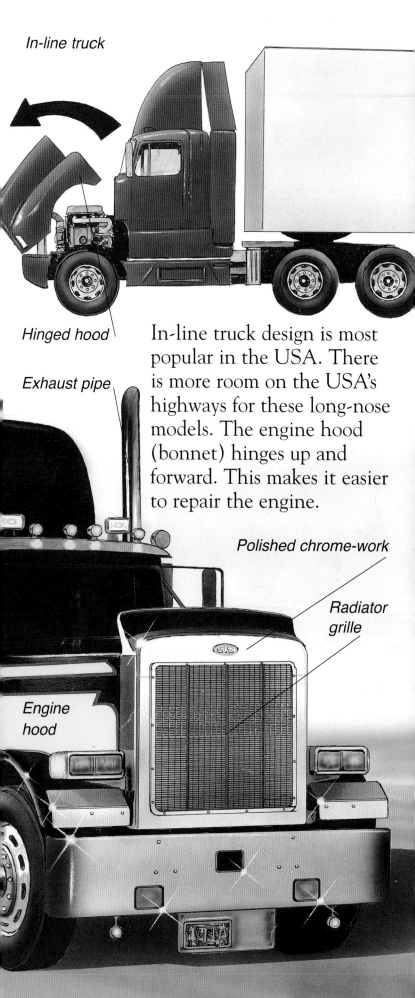

In-line truck

Hinged hood

Exhaust pipe

In-line truck design is most popular in the USA. There is more room on the USA's highways for these long-nose models. The engine hood (bonnet) hinges up and forward. This makes it easier to repair the engine.

Polished chrome-work

Radiator grille

Engine hood

An in-line truck has a long hood that cuts down the driver's view of the road. This is not a big problem on the open road but it makes it difficult to drive in busy towns. A cab-over truck has the driver's cab above the engine. This gives the driver a better view. The whole driver's cab tips forward to get to the engine. Cab-over trucks are popular in Europe. This is because roads there are not as big or wide as roads in the USA.

Semi-trailer

Cab-over truck

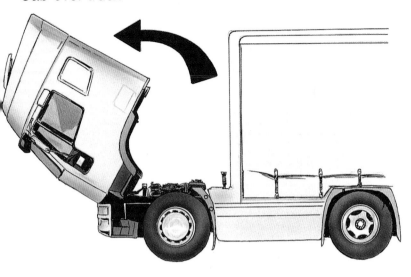

Tractor unit

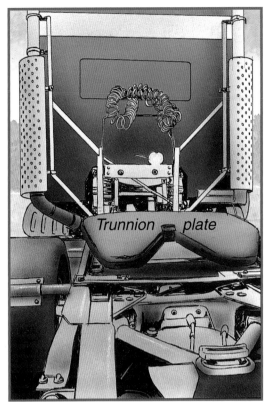

Trunnion plate

▲ To join the two parts of an articulated truck, the tractor reverses into the semi-trailer. A strong pin on the semi-trailer falls into place in the tractor's trunnion plate.

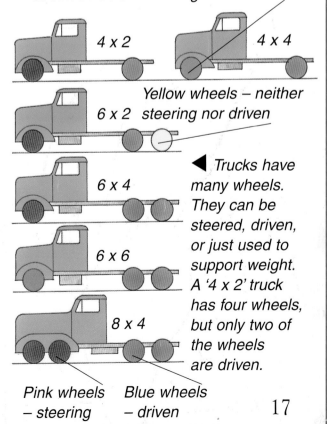

Green wheels – steering and driven

4 x 2   4 x 4

Yellow wheels – neither steering nor driven

6 x 2

6 x 4

◄ Trucks have many wheels. They can be steered, driven, or just used to support weight. A '4 x 2' truck has four wheels, but only two of the wheels are driven.

6 x 6

8 x 4

Pink wheels – steering   *Blue wheels – driven*

17

Tippers and Dumpers

Tipper trucks and dump trucks carry loose materials like earth or gravel. The back of the truck tips up to unload. It is lifted by engine-powered **hydraulic** rams.

Skip truck

Hydraulic arm

Skip

▲ A skip truck has two hydraulic arms. They can load and unload skips.

Forklift truck

▲ This modern forklift truck lifts and lowers its load like an ordinary forklift. It can also move its arm forwards to place a load onto a shelf.

▼ The Terex Titan is one of the world's biggest dump trucks. It can transport up to 550,000 kg at a time.

1927 Autocar tipper truck

Levers powered by engine

Hydraulic ram

▲ Early tipper trucks were raised by levers powered by the vehicle's small engine.

▼ A modern tipper can tip far heavier loads. Its hydraulic ram is much stronger. Its engine is much more powerful than earlier models.

Hydraulic arm

Steel
cables

Winch

WRECKER

Hydraulic
hoist

▼ The **hoist** operator of this
log truck uses hand controls to
move the hydraulic arm. The
grab closes and locks around
the logs. Then they are
lifted onto the truck.
Steel posts keep the
logs in place.

Steel
posts

Hoist
operator

Grab

20

◀ *A wrecker has a winch on a hydraulic arm at the back. It can lift a vehicle so that it can be towed away.*

Hydraulic rams

Decks

DUSTBIN LORRY

CAR TRANSPORTER

▲ *A car transporter has several decks that are supported by hydraulic rams. The rams lift the decks so cars can be driven on.*

▶ *Dustbin lorries have a compactor to squash rubbish. The rubbish in the hopper is crushed by a metal panel. The rubbish is then scooped into the truck.*

Hopper

Rubbish

Compactor

1

2

3

4

▲ *This shows how the compactor scoops the rubbish into the dustbin lorry's hopper.*

Military Trucks

M ilitary trucks transport soldiers and equipment. They have to be very reliable and easy to repair. Military trucks sometimes carry weapons. They have to be armour-plated for extra protection if they are used in combat zones.

▲ Military trucks were first used in large numbers during World War I (1914–1918). They often broke down and their thin wheels sank into the mud.

GMC CCKW 353

◀ The General Motors GMC CCKW 353 is an American military truck. More than half a million of them were made after 1941.

Tank transporter

Battle tank

▲ Battle tanks are moved by tank transporters. These powerful vehicles spread the weight of a tank to prevent damaging the road.

▶ An army road crane, the Scania P113 HK, is used to rescue vehicles. It has a ring on the roof of the cab to mount a machine-gun. It also has a winch.

AM General M923

▶ An AM General M923 truck tows a howitzer (a type of gun). The driver can change the air pressure of the tyres from inside the truck.

Howitzer

Tank engine

Caterpillar tracks

▲ A military crane replaces a tank's heavy engine. The crane's **caterpillar tracks** stop it sinking into soft ground.

Machine-gun mount

SCANIA P113 HK
ARMY ROAD CRANE

SCANIA

113 H   310

65416

23

Fire Engines

Early 17th-century fire engines were hand-operated water-pumps on wheels. Modern ones have equipment such as hydraulic ladders and elevator platforms. They help fire-fighters to tackle a variety of rescue operations.

Elevated platform

Hydraulic arm

Fire hydrant

▲ *This 1903 Merryweather Fire King was driven by a steam engine. The engine powered the water pump too.*

▼ *This petrol-driven model has a hose reel and a wheeled escape ladder.*

24

At the scene of a fire, water is collected from nearby fire **hydrants**. The truck's engine pumps the water into the hoses. The fire-fighters spray the fire with water. They can also use the engine's raised platform to spray the fire from different positions. A hydraulic arm can move the platform up or down.

1952 Crown Firecoach

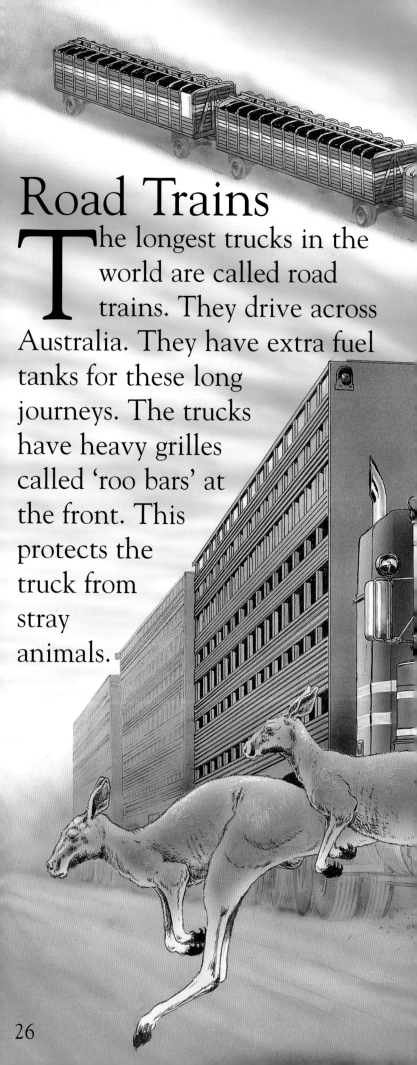

Road Trains

The longest trucks in the world are called road trains. They drive across Australia. They have extra fuel tanks for these long journeys. The trucks have heavy grilles called 'roo bars' at the front. This protects the truck from stray animals.

Road Trains can take deliveries from Sydney to Darwin.

Darwin

Australia

Sydney

Roo bars

TRAIN

▲ Airports have their own fire and rescue services. Airport fires may involve aviation fuel, so the fire engines spray foam instead of water.

▶ This hydraulic ladder is mounted on a rotating base. It can be turned and raised in any direction.

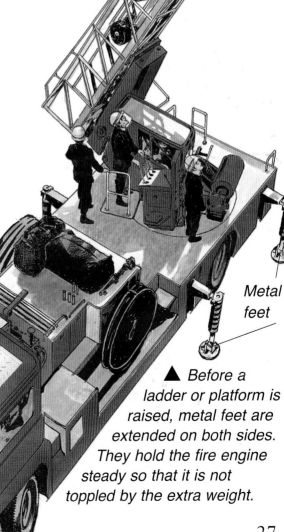

Metal feet

▲ Before a ladder or platform is raised, metal feet are extended on both sides. They hold the fire engine steady so that it is not toppled by the extra weight.

Trucks to Come

Trucks of the future need to be environmentally friendly. **Streamlined** trucks use less fuel because they create less air resistance. Future trucks may use a clean fuel such as **hydrogen**. It doesn't pollute the air with toxic fumes.

Prototype for multi-drop delivery truck

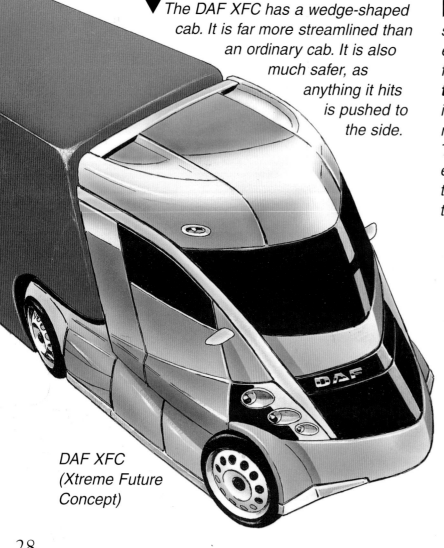

▼ The DAF XFC has a wedge-shaped cab. It is far more streamlined than an ordinary cab. It is also much safer, as anything it hits is pushed to the side.

DAF XFC
(Xtreme Future
Concept)

▶ Volvo's ECT was designed to show that trucks could be environmentally friendly. It has a **gas-turbine engine** instead of diesel to reduce air pollution. The engine powers electric motors that drive the wheels.

Volvo ECT
(Environmental
Concept Truck)

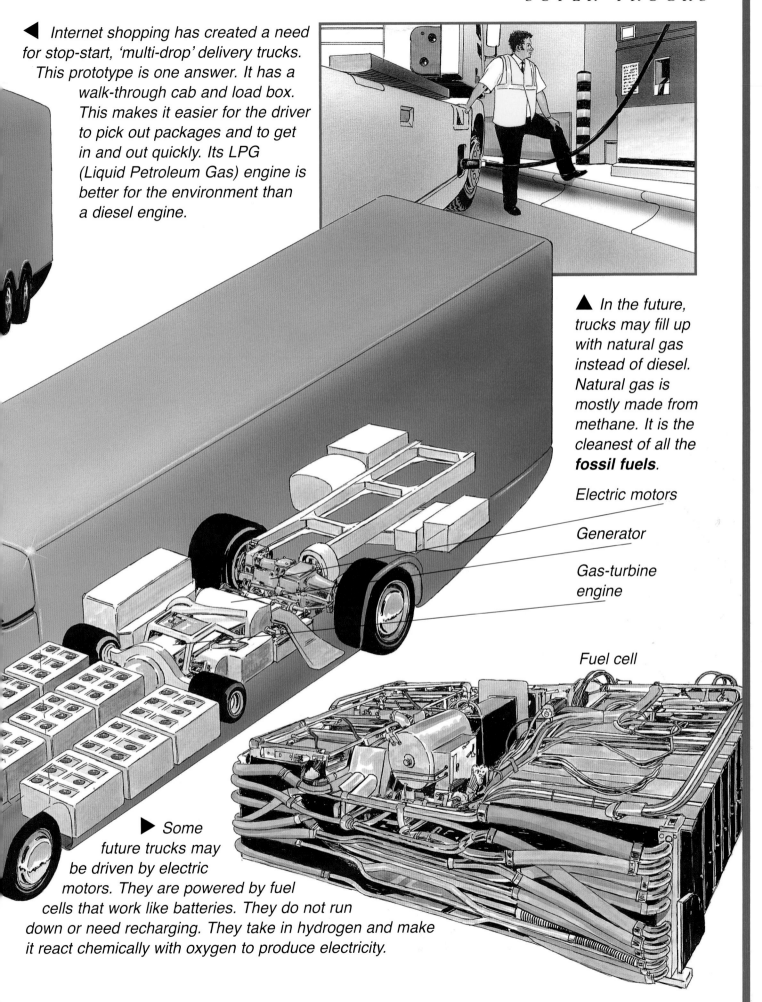

◄ Internet shopping has created a need for stop-start, 'multi-drop' delivery trucks. This prototype is one answer. It has a walk-through cab and load box. This makes it easier for the driver to pick out packages and to get in and out quickly. Its LPG (Liquid Petroleum Gas) engine is better for the environment than a diesel engine.

▲ In the future, trucks may fill up with natural gas instead of diesel. Natural gas is mostly made from methane. It is the cleanest of all the **fossil fuels**.

Electric motors

Generator

Gas-turbine engine

Fuel cell

► Some future trucks may be driven by electric motors. They are powered by fuel cells that work like batteries. They do not run down or need recharging. They take in hydrogen and make it react chemically with oxygen to produce electricity.

Useful Words

Air resistance
The amount of air that pushes against the vehicle as it moves.

Cab
The covered compartment of a truck for the driver to sit in.

Caterpillar tracks
A series of metal plates linked together and fitted around a heavy vehicle's wheels.

Chassis
The rectangular frame that holds the engine and wheels of a vehicle.

Diesel
A type of engine invented by the German engineer Rudolf Diesel.

Fire hydrant
A powerful tap that supplies water for fire-fighting.

Fossil fuels
Natural fuels such as coal and gas which were formed millions of years ago from the remains of living organisms.

Freight
Goods that are carried by different forms of transport.

Gas-turbine engine
A type of engine that burns fuel to produce gas. A turbine is a finned wheel which is turned by the force of the gas pushing against the fins.

Hoist
A lifting device or machine.

Hydraulic
Operated by pressurised fluid.

Hydrogen
A colourless, odourless and tasteless gas.

Pneumatic
Air-filled.

Prototype
The first model of a vehicle. It is used to test its design before it goes into production.

Streamlined
Made in a smooth, curved shape to reduce air resistance.

Tractor
A vehicle used to pull heavy loads, such as the cab and engine units that pull articulated trucks.

Vanes
Rigid surfaces which are used to turn fluid.

Winch
A motor-driven drum used to lift things by winding rope or cable around the drum.

Milestones

1769 French military engineer Nicolas Cugnot builds a steam tractor that can travel at 3.6 kph (2.2 mph).

1784 Scotsman William Murdock builds a working model of a steam-powered carriage.

1815 Scottish engineer John McAdam invents a new road surface called tarmacadam made from crushed rock and tar.

1845 Scotsman Robert William Thomson invents the rubber tyre.

1863 Jean-Joseph-Etienne Lenoir builds the first vehicle powered by an internal combustion engine instead of a steam engine.

1888 Scotsman John Boyd Dunlop invents the pneumatic (air-filled) rubber tyre.

1892 French engineer Rudolf Diesel invents a new type of engine, the diesel engine, that will later power trucks and other commercial vehicles.

1902 Drum brakes and disc brakes, the two types of brakes used by modern trucks, are invented.

1903 The first petrol-fuelled fire engine is introduced.

1908 The first twin wheels for trucks are introduced. A twin wheel is two wheels on the same axle instead of one.

1915 Detroit blacksmith August Fruehauf invents the tractor trailer, a truck with a separate driver's cab and trailer.

1916 4,500 trucks, buses and ambulances help to transport four million French troops to defend Verdun in France, during World War I.

1921 The first motorway is built in Germany.

1930 English engineer Bernard Dicksee builds a diesel engine that can be used by road vehicles. The 8.1-litre, six-cylinder engine is fitted in trucks.

1941 The first Jeep, a general purpose military vehicle, is introduced.

2006 Joint Venture Racing sets a truck speed record of 368 kph (229 mph).

2008 Caterpillar plans to develop a robotic control system for the largest truck in the world, the Caterpillar 797B.

Index

A

air pollution 28
airport tugs 8, 9
AM General M923 23
articulated trucks 9,
    14–17, 30
Autocar 6–7, 19

B

battle tanks 22, 23

C

cabs 6, 9, 14, 16, 22, 28,
    29, 30
cars 8, 9, 10, 21
car transporters 21
Caterpillar 797B 31
caterpillar tracks 23, 30
chassis 8, 9, 30
Chevrolet 7
chrome-work 15
concrete-mixer trucks
    12–13
construction industry
    12–13
Craftsman trucks 10
cranes 13, 22, 23

D

DAF XFC 28
Daimler 6
delivery trucks 9, 28, 29
drawbar-trailer outfits 8
dump trucks 13, 18, 30
dustbin lorries 21

E

electricity 29
electric motors 28, 29
engines 8, 9, 11, 15, 16,
    18, 19, 23, 24, 25, 28,
    29, 30, 31
environment 28, 29
exhaust pipes 15

F

fire engines 24–25, 27, 31
forklift truck 18
fuel 8, 26, 27, 28, 29, 30,
    31
fuel cells 29
fuel tanks 26

H

hoists 20, 30
hydrants 24, 25
hydraulic
    arms 18, 20, 21, 24, 25
    hoists 20
    ladder 27
    rams 18, 19, 21
hydrogen 28, 29, 30

J

Jeep 31
Joint Venture Racing 31

L

Lacre 7
log trucks 20–21

M

military trucks 22–23

P

prototypes 28, 29, 30

R

racing trucks 10, 11
radiator grilles 15
recovery trucks 8, 9
rigid trucks 9
road trains 26–27
'roo bars' 27

S

Scania P113 HK 22, 23
semi-trailers 14, 16
skip trucks 18

T

tank transporters 22
tankers 8
Terex Titan 18
tipper trucks 9, 18–19
tow trucks 8
tractor units 10, 14, 17, 30
trailers 8, 10, 17
truck racing 10–11
trunnion plate 17
tyres 6, 7, 23, 31

V

Volvo ECT 28–29

W

wheelies 10
wheels 7, 17, 22, 24, 28,
    30,
winches 8, 20, 21, 22, 30
World War I 22, 31
wreckers 20–21